SCRIPTURAL THEMES

By
ARTHUR GREENE

First Fruits Press
Wilmore, Kentucky
c2017

Scriptural themes.
By Arthur Greene.

First Fruits Press, ©2017
Previously published by the Pentecostal Publishing Company, ©1936.

ISBN: 9781621717492 (print) 9781621717508 (digital),

Digital version at http://place.asburyseminary.edu/firstfruitsheritagematerial/143/

For all other uses, contact:

First Fruits Press
B.L. Fisher Library
Asbury Theological Seminary
204 N. Lexington Ave.
Wilmore, KY 40390
http://place.asburyseminary.edu/firstfruits

Greene, Arthur.

Scriptural themes / by Arthur Greene. Wilmore, Kentucky: First Fruits Press, ©2017.

89 pages: portrait; 21 cm.

Reprint. Previously published: North Attleboro, Mass.: Pillar of Fire, ©1909.

Contents: A cloud of witnesses -- Holiness, supremely excellent -- Glory of the spiritual body -- Religious infidelity -- Post-millennial heresy -- The authority of scripture -- The voice of judgement -- The golden age -- Towards the great divine event -- The image of God restored -- The glory of Christ's kingdom -- Signs of Christs speedy coming -- New life in Jesus -- The gracious invitation.

ISBN - 13: 979781621717492 (pbk.)

1. Theology, Doctrinal--Popular works. I. Title.

BT77.G73 2016

Cover design by Jon Ramsay

asburyseminary.edu
800.2ASBURY
204 North Lexington Avenue
Wilmore, Kentucky 40390

First Fruits
THE ACADEMIC OPEN PRESS OF ASBURY SEMINARY

First Fruits Press
The Academic Open Press of Asbury Theological Seminary
204 N. Lexington Ave., Wilmore, KY 40390
859-858-2236
first.fruits@asburyseminary.edu
asbury.to/firstfruits

Arthur Greene.

Scriptual Themes.

— BY —

ARTHUR GREENE.

PRESIDENT OF "BIBLE HOME AND FOREIGN MISSION-
ARY SOCIETY," EDITOR OF "THE PILLAR OF FIRE,"
AUTHOR OF TRACTS "WHOSOEVER,' "GOD'S TIME
NOW," 'TWO WORKS," "THE CHURCH," "PEACE,"
"FOREVER LOST," 'A HOLY LIFE," "A REPLY TO
AN OPPOSER OF HOLINESS," "THE HOLY
CITY," THE BANQUET," "A TRUE INCI-
DENT." AND MANY OTHERS OF NOTE.

1909

'THE PILLAR OF FIRE"

NORTH ATTLEBORO, MASS.

TO THE MEMBERS
OF THE FIRST EMMANUEL
CHURCH AND THE MEMBERS OF
THE PEOPLES' FREE CHURCH WHO
HAVE STOOD FOR THE WHOLE TRUTH OF
GOD THRO STORM AND TEMPEST
THIS BOOK IS AFFECTIONATE-
LY DEDICATED BY THE
A U T H O R.

NAMES OF PERSONS WHOSE VIEWS ON THESE TOPICS
ARE QUOTED:

EMMONS.	KNAPP.	D'AUBIGNE
EDWARDS.	SIMMONS.	BAXTER.
MACLAREN.	SPURGEON,	STEBBINS

Table of Contents.

A Cloud of Witnesses.

---✠---

THERE is no one subject that has claimed the same amount of attention among the great army of Bible students as the one under consideration. Christian perfection is the great, prominent, and eternal fact in the salvation of souls, as set forth in the Bible. Jesus Christ, our example in all things, taught that it was the pure in heart that should see God. (Matt. v, 8.) Moses, the man chosen by the highest authority to govern the people of God, anciently, taught them the necessity of experimental holiness. "Sanctify yourselves therefore, and be ye holy; for I am the Lord your God," (Lev. xx, 7.) The Psalmist, unobstructedly sets forth the fact that holiness is essential to worship

7

God. "Who shall ascend into the hill of the Lord? or who shall stand in His holy place? He that hath clean hands, and a pure heart; who hath not lifted up his soul unto vanity, nor sworn deceitfully." (Psa. xxiv, 3-4.) The Apostle Paul, under the inspiration of the Holy Ghost, wrote to the Ephesian church, that we were chosen before the foundation of the world, to be holy and without blame before Him in love. (Eph. i, 4.) Thus we see the scriptures are a unit upon this all-important theme.

All God's children should see eye to eye concerning christian experience. "Irony, sarcasm, and ridicule should have small place in the literature of love." This great central truth of holy christianity, in sermon and testimony, should be kept before the members of Christ's flock, as their privilege. G. E. Ackerman of the U. S. Grant University, says, "The deepest emotions of the soul are voiceless." "The deepest experiences refuse to be defined." How true the proverb—"It is better felt than told."

"The implantation of spiritual life does not destroy the carnal mind; though its power is broken, it does not cease to exist.

While the new birth is the beginning of purification, it is perhaps, more the process of imparting or begetting spiritual life, than the process of refining or purification, which in entire sanctification is the extraction of remaining impurity from regenerated human nature." Bishop Hedding says—"That a soul merely born of God needs a further sanctification is evident from the whole current of the Apostles' teaching." Mr. Wesley says—"Imbred sin may exist where it does not reign." "The justified soul strives against these corruptions, does not allow them, hates them, mourns over them, and groans under them as a burden, and seeks their destruction or removal." "We are informed that man was made in the image of God. We infer, then, that intellect, sensibility, and will, in man, are the same in kind as in God. The differance is quantitative, not qualitative. If this inferance be valid—and it has never yet been invalidated—it must follow that justice, goodness, righteousness, and holiness are the same kind in man as in God. The difference is in degree, not in essence." Dr. Dougan Clark adds his testimony to the already

9

growing cloud of witnesses upon this highly interesting theme—"Summing up these plain declarations of Holy Scripture, we find that we are sanctified by the blood of Christ; we are sanctified by the Holy Ghost; we are sanctified by the truth, and we are sanctified by faith. Nowhere do we read that we are sanctified by growth, nor that we are sanctified by death. Here, then, we might rest our argument, at least, until some shadow of scripture proof shall be produced, to show that by a gradual growth in grace we may at least attain to entire sanctification; or on the other hand, that only when the soul is leaving the body, can it be cleansed from all sin.

But are not the different modes by which entire sanctification is received, as quoted above, contradictory and self-destructive? Could not an opposer say to us: If a man is sanctified by the truth, he is not sanctified by faith; and if he is sanctified by faith, he is not sanctified by the Holy Ghost, and so on? We answer that the different expressions employed in reference to this glorious work, are perfectly consistent, and fit into each other with beautiful simplicity and accuracy. Each quotation is a part of the grand whole, and each presents one aspect of the great work, which is complete only when all are included. This we shall proceed with God's good help to demonstrate.

We are sanctified by the will of God; for we read in another place, "This is the will of God, even your sanctification." God's will is the expression of His grace. His grace is the expression of His love. "God so loved the world that He gave His only begotten Son." It is therefore God's love, or God's grace, or God's will that is the source of our sanctification. But all gospel blessings are procured for us by the atonement of Christ. He "of God is made unto us wisdom, and righteousness, and sanctification, and redemption." It follows then indubitably, that the blood of Jesus is the ground of our sanctification. Rev. John Fletcher in his "Last Check" says:—"The same spirit of faith which initially purifies our hearts when we cordially believe the pardoning love of God, completely cleanses them when we fully believe His sanctifying love." "But when I speak of the purifica-

11

tion of the heart (says Dr. Adam Clark) or doctrine of Christian Perfection, I use sanctification in the sense in which it is understood among Methodists." "What then is this complete sanctification?" It is the cleansing by the blood, that has not been cleansed; it is the washing of a true believer from the remains of sin.

Binney's Theological Compend defines holiness as—"That participation of the divine nature, which excludes all original depravity, or imbred sin from the heart"— entire sanctification is that act of the Holy Ghost whereby the justified soul is made holy.

The great American Lexicographer defines sanctification—"The act of making holy, * * * the state of being thus purified or sanctified." "To sanctify, (he says) in a general sense, is to cleanse, purify, or make holy, * * * to cleanse from corruption, to purify from sin."

Rev. Albert Barnes says: "To sanctify means to render pure, or to cleanse from sins. * * * Who seek not only to have the external actions correct, but who desire to be holy in heart, and are so. The general meaning is, that in regard to any and every sin of which we may be conscious, there is efficacy in the blood to remove it, and to make us wholly pure. There is no stain, that the blood of Christ cannot take it entirely away from the soul."

"As flowers their opening leaves display
   And glad drink in the solar fire,
So may we catch thy every ray,
   So may thy influence us inspire,
Thou beam of the eternal beam
   Thou purging fire, thou quickening flame."
                              —*Wesley.*

Holiness, Supremely Excellent.

---✠---

"HOLINESS is that which God supremely requires in all His commands. If there was anything more noble, or morally excellent than holiness, we might have expected that God would have required us to pursue that supremely, and holiness subordinately. But he has expressly commanded us to pursue holiness supremely and everything else in subordination to it." It is only because holiness is in its own nature, supremely valuable and excellent, that it may never be sacrificed, on any occasion or consideration whatever. If it had been right for Christians to sacrifice their holiness, thousands and thousands of

14

martyrs might have saved their lives, by only disavowing the truth, or denying the faith. But they wisely chose to sacrifice their lives rather than their holiness. It can never be right for any moral agent to sacrifice his holiness to promote any design, to obtain any good, or to avoid any evil.

But this is true, only on the supposition that holiness is intrinsically and supremely excellent. 'If holiness is not immeasurably more excellent, valuable, and important, than happiness, why should happiness be made a mere reward for holiness? And if sin is not an immeasurably greater and more hateful abominable evil, than mere misery, how can God be justified in visiting a single sinful action, with such protracted, complicated, and severe sufferings, and especially threatening probationary sins, with eternal punishment."

Dr. Emmons in writing upon this important subject says, — "Some things are valuable only as means, not as ends; but others are valuable as ends, and not as means. Bread and other kinds of food are valuable as means to preserve life; and good books are valuable as means to promote knowledge. But neither bread nor books would have any value, if the one did no feed the body, and the other the mind. They are not, therefore, valuable in their own nature. But holiness is morally excellent in its own nature, aside from all its happy effects and consequences. As it is intrinsically excellent, so it is supremely valuable. There is nothing in the universe equal to it in worth and importance."

"Holiness is the truth, glowing all over, webbing all through Revelation; the glorious truth which sparkles and whispers and sings and shouts in all its history, and biography, and poetry, and prophecy, and precept, and promise, and prayer; the great central truth of the system." "It is a philosophical as well as scripture truth that if Christ can save from sin at all, He can save from all sin. He can sanctify His people wholly, in body, soul, and spirit. He redeems such as trust in Him from all iniquity, fills them with all the fullness of God, keeps them from falling, and presents them faultless before His presence in glory with exceeding joy." "Holiness is the architectural plan upon which God buildeth up His living temple." Lady Huntington very beautifully expresses the state of her inner nature with these words—"My whole heart has not one single grain, this moment, of thirst after approbation. I feel alone with God; He fills the whole void; I have not one wish, one will, one desire, but in Him; He hath set my feet in a large room, I have wondered and stood amazed that God should make a conquest of all within me by love."

The testimony of George Fox breathes forth life, light and victory. These are his words:—"I knew Jesus, and he was very precious to my soul; but I found something within me that would not keep sweet and patient and kind. I did what I could to keep it down, but it was there. I besought Jesus to do something for me; and when I gave Him my will, He came and took out all that would not be sweet, and all that would not be kind, all that would not be patient, and then He shut the door."

James Brainerd Taylor, a Presbyterian minister, says that after his conversion he was greatly troubled on account of indwelling sin, but that finally he was lead into perfect peace. His own words are:—"My mind loves to dwell upon this delightful theme—holiness. It is a blessed doctrine. O why did I not come to possess it before? Why, because, like many other professors of religion, I looked for a death purgatory, not believing that the blood of Christ cleanseth from all sin. This is the present tense. It is efficacious now, and the Lord has proved to me a full, a complete Saviour."

"Believe in Jesus, art thou poor and friendless in the world, forced to say with the Redeemer whilst He was down here, 'The foxes have holes, the birds of the air have nests,' but I have not a home I can call my own in this whole world? Look up to Heaven, thy home, in faith and in hope. Oh, how rich is thy portion to be yonder forever. The Bible represents the glorified who are in Heaven as in a state of holiness. Their holiness is a very prominent feature in their present state of glory. 'Holiness unto the Lord,' was an inscription engraven upon the front of the mitre of the high priest in Israel: 'Holiness unto the Lord' is an inscription written, if I may use the expression, by the finger of the Holy Spirit upon

18

the brow of the glorified soul, and upon the crown that is placed there."

Heaven is a world of perfect holiness: it is God's Holy of Holies, the most awfully sacred and solemn place in His whole universe. The preparation for Heaven is thus set forth in the scriptures by one emphatic sentence—"Holiness, without which no man shall see the Lord." Not only do the scriptures set forth christian holiness as an attainable state, or blessing—distinct from and subsequent to justification—but a fair interpretation of several passages of scripture bring this interesting state before our minds as susceptible of a perpetually increasing beauty and finish. Such are the following: "He will beautify the meek with salvation." "Perfecting holiness in the fear of the Lord." "O worship the Lord in the beauty of holiness." Holiness is having the heart cleansed, and sanctified by the spirit, and filled with love to God, and all mankind. It is love, in thought, word, and action.

But here we see that "holiness" may be "perfected"—"meekness" may be "beautified"—and a certain state or degree of

19

christian experience is described as the "beauty of holiness." This illustrates and substantiates the interesting truth, that christian holiness does not preclude a growth in grace, or an increase in spiritual attainments. Our purity of heart may be garnished by the influence of the Spirit, until like the highly polished steel, it reflects the image of Christ, not only with accuracy, but with beauty. Our love—the main channel of which flows to God, and becomes a regulator to the smaller ones, and is therefore considered perfect—may receive additional lustre and beauty, in an increasing strength—the uniformity of its exercise— and the harmony of various channels. Holiness is beautiful, but it may be beautified. The heart may not only be "cleansed from all sin"—"swept and garnished"—but polished, till, like the king's daughter, it is "all glorious within." This is the "Beauty of Holiness." How reasonable to expect that the King of Heaven would adorn and beautify His mansion and dwelling place; and how well-founded are our desires and expectations of becoming the polished temples of the living God; for He says "ye are the temple of the living God;" as He saith, I will dwell in them; and walk in them; and "I will be their God and they shall be my people."

"I lay my sins on Jesus,
   The spotless Lamb of God ;
 He bears them all, and frees us
   From the accursed load.
 I bring my guilt to Jesus,
   To wash my crimson stains
 White in His blood most precious,
   Till not a spot remains."

Glory of the Spiritual Body.

---✠---

"WHO can put on a sad countenance, and speak in desponding tones of the great change that is coming? Surely it is not becoming to the christian thus to demean himself when every step of his progress is from glory to glory. The change is, indeed, great for him, but it is also glorious. It is transformation, but upon every feature of it is written exaltation in living characters. The blessed perfection he will know in the world of light will most emphatically be unlike the imperfection he once knew, the joyous freedom very different from his former bondage, and all his re-

22

lations in striking and delightful contrast with all that was previously known.

A body that pleases God must be transcendently glorious—a structure of inconceivable beauty; and such have all His saints. Whatever pleases God will please them; therefore, what harmony and appreciation will exist among the ranks of the blessed! There will be no disturbing influence to effect those refined organizations; nothing can deface the "image of the Heavenly," for the source of its brightness is ever present to keep it undimmed forever. There is no friction—no blight—no decay to come near the glorified bodies which the ransomed possess. What then is their power?

While within the precints of mortality, the spirit is repressed in its efforts, restrained in its endeavors, by the influence of encircling matter; but in the land of immortality it shall be different—spirit sha'l triumph over everything else—it will be supreme. If it have a "body," this will aid the spirit effectually in all its movements and designs—there will be no limitations, or restraints whatever. All that is conceived

in the idea of freedom will be realized in
the union; and, all that we can associate
with the idea of power is experienced also.
It is sin that prevents the harmonizing of
the elements of power in this world—that
hinders the efficiency of concentrated forces
in worthy and benevolent enterprises—that
throws difficulties and obstacles in the way
of the chariot of salvation, and before those
whose guiding hand would make a way for
it in all the earth. It is sin that makes the
individual so powerless in vanquishing the
foes which threaten his destruction, that
makes him so weak when assailed by those
that are ever lying in wait to entice him
away from the path of self-denial, which
must be traversed to get to the Holy City,
and toward which he is looking, half wish-
ing that he were there. It is sin that keeps
one so long halting "between two opinions,"
causing him to lie down on an uneasy
couch, and awake to a restless knowledge
day by day, without the power to throw
down the burden and escape from the press-
ure. It is sin that prevents the wavering
one from breaking over the customs and
prejudices of an "evil and gainsaying
24

world," from laying aside its trammels and chains, with a fixed and final determination to be henceforth guided by the Infinite One —to be influenced by considerations from above and beyond all that is earthy and transitory. In these workings of sin there is a want of moral power. In the decision involving obedience there is a divinely granted power. In the determination to live a life of faith, and walk in the ways of holiness, a power is delegated from above. But there is a painful deficiency in this power while wielded by fleshly weapons— not in the thing itself, but from a want where it falls. Power, as such, in the fullest and richest extent, its varied and all-conquering nature—we mean, as God-communicated,—is found alone in Heaven, in the glorified bodies of the redeemed. Creature-power culminates there. The disturbing forces of sin are never present to distract and confound, to cause a failure in the slightest degree. His chosen ones even reign—though with the mildest authority, yet most potent in sway—they are "kings and priests" there, and exercise most benignant rule over all, in the sphere to which they are called.

25

The soul naturally loves power; it craves it, seeks it sometimes, yea, oftentimes, for base ends, but rightly seeking it from holiest motive, it shall be given, even in this life, as an earnest of that which shall be vested in the glorified being hereafter. That which is "sown in weakness" "will be raised in power." This will be an element of the spiritual being, and not to be comprehended in its blissful application now — power, it may be, to go to the ends of the earth on the holiest errand, on the most loving mission; power, it may be, to go to other worlds to tell of love divine, love redeeming —to witness wonderful displays of creative skill; power, it may be, to plan and execute great and noble deeds; but, at least, a power to do God's will and pleasure forever. And is not this an inexpressible delight, O Christian, encompassed with the infirmities of the flesh, struggling against sin, and longing to be free from its entanglements —with a desire that excells all others in strength and constancy? But the body is not only "raised in power"—it is "raised in glory" also; and how expressive this word as used by the sacred writers! not beauty,

26

not excellence simply, but glory, transcent brightness, a brilliancy surpassing mortal conception. Who can tell the meaning of the scripture phrase, "full of glory," or comprehend what was intended by "glory, honor, and immortality," or analyze and bring out plain to the understanding what it is to be "glorified with Him," even Christ? These are the things to be learned in God's eternal school, under His direct and blessed teaching: these are the things to be observed when, standing in the holy ranks, the brightness of the Heavenly host is everywhere reflected. Fashioned like unto His most glorious body is the promise; His body is the pattern; and what ideas does it suggest of beauty and symmetry, of fullness and perfection !

The invisible gives place to the visible, and clouds and darkness no more hide, or obscure in any sence, the beauty of the soul; for that 'which is perfect is come." The beauty of holiness expands into glory, revealing itself in the sun-lit countenance of the ransomed, becoming the unutterable, the inexpressible of our present ideas. As Christ was "altogether" "lovely," so will

also the glorified saint be in the day of resurrection glory; for he has bathed himself
in the clear stream issuing from Calvary, and
come forth with neither a spot, nor a stain,
nor a blemish. He bears the l keness of the
Saviour—that perfect and satisfying likeness
which so many have coveted to possess.   In
what strange contrast will that be with the
image of the earthly,—that image so often
marred and defaced by the marks of sin,—
that image in which it was often so diffi-
cult to trace the linements of the divine !
How different will be the glorified body
from that miserable, pain-distressed form
which disease crushed, until no more re-
mained for it but to moulder in the dust, an
inanimate and lifeless thing !   The one is
unsightly and forbidding; the other immortal, beautiful, yea, glorious, reflecting the
indescribable glory of the Eternal, and
bearing about with it the unearthly lustre
of the skies.   This is the goal to which
holy ambition always turns; for this christians willingly die.   The purely spiritual
dwells inside the golden gates of the "New
Jerusalem."   Those who walk there have
glorified bodies—bodies in which are vested

power, honor and glory; bodies that are incorruptible and spiritual; and those who have the requisite seal will yet pass in, and receive for their everlasting service these same glorious vestments, that are not made after any human pattern, but with devices wrought out by the King of Kings—the Lord of Heaven. This, O Christian, belongs to thine inheritance!"

"Oh City where the shining gates
    Shut out all grief and sin !
Well may we yearn, amid earth's strife,
    The holy place to win.
Yet we must meekly bear the cross,
    Nor seek to lay it down,
Until our Farther brings us home,
    And gives the promised crown,"

Religious Infidelity.

———✠———

THAT there is much unbelief even among professing christians is a fact so well known that we do not have to prove it. Webster, in giving the definition of infidelity says: "In general, want of faith or belief, a withholding of credit. Disbelief of the inspiration of the Scriptures, or the divine origin of christianity. Unbelief." It is seen at once that the backbone of Infidelity is summed up in one word—Unbelief. There is no doubt, a large number of professing christians who style themselves honest doubters, will object to being called an infidel.

The first trace of this form of subtle infidelity was seen in the garden of Eden when the Devil told the woman "ye shall

not surely die." It's effects are too well
known to call forth an elaborate argument
to prove the same. The fact stands, that
unbelief was the cause of our first parents
outward sin. If they had continued to believe that God meant what He said, they never would have disobeyed Him. The popular
notion that is so prominent in this age—
that each one has a perfect right to sit in
judgment upon God's word, and receive
what they like, and refuse all that does not
meet their approval is to say the least,
measuring God by the finite mind. This is
one of the many forms of religious infidelity. The Bible as a whole is the word of
God; if not, then we are at sea without
chart or compass. If the Bible contains as
some would have us believe, inspired and un-
inspired writings, who is the one to
determine which is, and which is not inspired? To prove that any single book of the
inspired record is not the word of God is
sufficient cause to doubt it all. D'Aubigne
in his book on the "Authority of God" clearly sets forth in beautiful language his faith
in the sacred writings—the following is
taken from the same:

"The principle of eternal life which is infused into you when you are converted, and which, alas! is still so imperfect, is not assuredly of human origin, It is God, yes, God Himself, who is the Author of it. To testify that it is God, and not man, who has converted you, you would be ready to lay down your lives. Is not this true, children of God? What then! are those scriptures, wherein is found a Divine life far more pure, more perfect, more original, and more natural, than that which dwells in our poor hearts,—are they of human origin? What! is God not their Author! Ah! if I acknowledge the hand of God, and the Spirit of God, in a little hillock, with much more reason do I recognize them in the snow-clad and gigantic masses of the Alps. If I recognize the hand of God, and the Spirit of God, in the humming-bee, much stronger reason exists for me to recognize them in the majestic countenance of man. If I recognize the hand of God, and the Spirit of God, in that new light which dawns in my heart, much more abundant cause have I to recognize them in that creative light which beams in tne 'Holy Scriptures,' and which

32

lighteth every man that cometh into the world.' (John i, 9.) Thus then, my brethren, that Holy Spirit which some wish to exalt to the exclusion of the Authority of the Scriptures, does itself testify to the Divine authority of the oracles of God." Our faith in the word of God is not a faith simply historic, as some imagine; nor a faith purely philosophic, as others dream; no, it is a Divine faith,—a faith which carries with it a certainty;—an innate stability; elevated, immovable, as God the Author of it. This being a fact, we, as the children of God, are happy in our belief of the Sacred Word.

He who disbelieves any portion of the Sacred Word, does so at his peril. To say there is no everlasting punishment is equivalent to calling God a liar. To disbelieve in the blood that cleanses the heart from all sin is to take sides with the devil against Christ. To say that Jesus is not going to return and reign upon this earth is to advertise infidelity. "Friends and brethren, I am at a loss at which to wonder most: whether at the severity of Almighty God upon the finally impenitent, or at the un-

33

concern, neglect, and hardihood of men, who, with all this dreadful outcome before their eyes, still march calmly on in the very path which can have no other termination, —O how dreadful! Retreat to the Lazerhouse to refresh one's self with the groans and miseries of the wretched, a dance in the chamber of death, the singing of glees around the coffin of a beloved and honored friend, the making of merry jests over the fresh grave of one's own dear mother, would not be half so unseemly, so unfeeling, and so insane, as to go on in a life of indifference and impenitence, with eyes open and ears informed of all the horrible consequences which must come of it! There is but one explanation,—people do not half believe. They profess to receive and honor the Bible, but they do not credit what it so plainly says. They would feel indignant and resentful were we to call them infidels, and yet they are infidels; They may not speak the infidel's creed, but they live it every day, an l think well of themselves whilst they do it." "The inner temper of their souls—their spiritual tone—is infidel. The practical spirit which influences and controlls them is the infidel spirit, and accords with the infidel reasoning. Either they do not think at all, and so reduce themselves to the level of the irrational brute; or their thinking is secretly, if not confessedly, tinged with the suspicion that these mighty revelations are nothing but unsubstantial speculation, or doubtful theory. They have a deep persuasion of the certainty, regularity, and permanence of what they call natural laws, and have schooled themselves into such a trust and confidence and worship of nature, that they see no need, or likelihood, or possibility of any other divinity, or divine administrations.

Thunder, lightning, tempests, comets, at which mankind once trembled as signs of God's angry interference with human affairs, they find so largely explainable on natural principles, that they are slow to admit that God has anything to do with these things, or that He is able to use them as His weapons of Judgment. They talk of God, but to them He is an impotent God. Consciously or unconsciously, their souls are thus in a condition of skepticism, which empties the Divine Word of all reality to them. They hear it, and see what it says, but have a lingering feeling that it cannot be true just as it reads, and so pass it by as a dead letter. O ye people of earthly wisdom, be not deceived! Where there are such effective laws as you speak of, there must needs be an Almighty Lawgiver who made and put them into force, and He who could make them, can also unmake and modify them as he pleases. Is efficient government any less the administration of Sovereign power because it acts through great, settled, and well-known laws? Is His majesty disabled by having shown Himself so great? What is more irrational than rationalism? Is God helpless to fulfill His word because He in nature proves Himself Almighty? Hath He made the blunder of binding His hands with His own Omnipotence? Such would seem to be the essence of some men's reasoning.

Post=Millennial Heresy.

—✠—

MAY this feeble article, by the grace of Christ, be at least a single stone suitable to form part of that bulwark which should be raised in this country against the double aggression of the higher critic and Post-Millennialism! Every loyal soul to God's Bible as a whole should now employ himself in endeavoring to strengthen this bulwark, "as in the days of Ezra and Nehemiah, he should have the trowel in one hand, and the sword in the other." "They who pretend to throw down this bulwark have with them, it is true, some divines of the declining Church," "but they who wish to uphold it have on their side the Apostles and the Lord Himself." 'The Church ought to mark well the manner in

37

which it's Divine Head expelled the enemy."

What is the first weapon which it behooves us to employ in our wrestling with the adversary? "The Lord answers: 'The Scriptures.'" Do we again ask, what is the second? the Scriptures. * * · and the third?—the Scriptures." Please notice! we are to meet the adversary with the Scriptures as a whole, and not a fractional part of the same. Paul, in writing to Timothy, emphatically states that ·'All Scripture is given by inspiration of God, and is profitable for doctrine, for reproof, for correction, for instruction in righteousness: That the *Man of God* may be perfect, thoroughly furnished unto all good works." (2 Tim. iii, 16-17.)

"The Christ of the Bible and the Bible of the Christ are month after month increasingly rejected. The darkness of apostasy into which the professing masses of Christendom are rushing, is fearful. What an evidence this fact is in itself of the inspiration of the Bible, for it has clearly predicted every phase of the present day falling away from the faith!" 'Lo, they have rejected the word of the Lord, and what wisdom is in them." (Jer. viii. 9.) "This is the root of the whole matter, they have rejected the word of the Lord." "The Bible has been most subtly undermined by men who style themselves 'honest critics,' or claimed to be occupied with 'reverend higher criticism.'" The schools of higher criticism are so closely related in their work, that it is hard to tell which the Devil is using to the best advantage. One denies the Authority of the Bible, while the other declares that it does not mean what it says. Peter makes mention of both these classes in his Second Epistle and third chapter. "And account that the long-suffering of our Lord is salvation; even as our beloved brother Paul also according to the wisdom given unto him hath written unto you. As also in all his Epistles, speaking in them of these things, in which are some things hard to be understood, which they that are unlearned, and unstable *Wrest*, as they do also the other Scriptures unto their own destruction. Ye therefore beloved, seeing ye know these things before, beware lest ye also, being led away with the errors of the wicked, fall from your own steadfastness." (2 Pet. iii,

39

15-16-17.) At this particular point we are brought face to face with the Authority of God as revealed in His word. Who is he who dare mutilate or wrest that which bears the seal of All-Mighty God? Both the Old Testament and the New alike contain the infallible word of the Living God.

We are fully aware of the fact, that we expose ourselves to the guns of the enemy, as we contend for the faith once delivered unto the saints; not a portion of faith, but "The Faith"—which embraces all revealed Truth.

"The New Testament, which essentially announces to us not the law, but the gospel, and which announces it to us not by images and prophecies more or less obscure, but with a great abundance of light and brightness; The New Testament which makes us know Him who is above all prophets and kings of the Old Covenant, Him, from whose fullness we receive grace and truth, —the New Testament, which not only removes the veil that prevented the prophets from arriving at a clear view of those things which they foretold, but which further makes manifest "the mystery,

40

which was kept secret since the world began." (Rom. xvi 20.) This New Testament ought evidently to be the foundation, the rule, the testimony, and the divine authority upon which christian knowledge should rest. It is the first and essential source of evangelical truth, and if God himself is the *Rock* whence issue the less clear waters of the "Old Covenant," it would be illogical and anti-christian to attribute another origin to the pure and life-giving streams of the new revelation. The Old Testament is like the first table-land of our Alps, the ground of which is firm and the view from it extensive, but which are in reality the ladder steps, to enable us to reach those lofty heights from which we can behold the immensity of the Creator's works. In passing from one to the other you do not descend, but mount; you do not tread on ground less stable, but on a resting-place more firm.

If as has been clearly shown the Old and New Testaments are to be relied upon as authoritative, then we make no mistake in sounding forth the Truths which they contain. The unscriptural ground taken by those who oppose the doctrine of Christ's speedy return will soon be swept away by the glory of His Presence.

Just as the Antedeluvians would not heed the preaching of Noah, so there are those who will not accept the "Full Gospel Message." But whether they will or not, let us consider that the great mass of humanity are engulfed in the maelstron of sin, which is sweeping its millions down to graves of destruction, (Matt. vii, 13.) and compared to them, in numbers, the true believers are but a handful. If the world is to be converted before Jesus comes as the Post-Millennial teachers affirm, about how many years will it take to convert the world and of what force would the words of the Saviour be: "What I say unto you I say unto *All*, Watch,"? Do you not see at once that the words of Jesus would be the greatest riddle in history if the Post-Millennial theory was correct, for what sense would there be in telling His followers to watch for His Coming, and in another discourse tell them the world must be converted before He Comes?

It is said that taking the position that the Pre-Millennial teachers do, proves the gospel a failure. But this is not so—Man is a failure. The gospel is the power of God unto Salvation to every one that believeth. (Rom i, 6.) "I is not the incompetency of the gospel, but the willful unbelief of sinners that prevents the evangelization of the world. It is objected that this doctrine presents a gloomy view of the future—that "it is the philosophy of despair"—that it stands opposed to the popular idea; e. g. that the world is growing better, and if it is true, it is sarcastically said, "we might as well fold our hands and wait for Christ to come." We candidly think that many who raise these objections, have altogether mistaken the spirit and work of the Pre-Millenialists." We neither despair, nor fold our hands to sleep. On the contrary, we are filled with a lively hope, while we strive to save some from this worldly, sinful, and adulterous generation, which is nigh unto cursing, and whose end is to be burned. (Gal. i, 4; Heb. vi, 8; Mal. iv, 1.) We would not deceive them with the hallucination that they are "growing better," for, as the Apostle has said, "we know that we are of God and the whole world lieth in wickedness." (1 John v, 19.) Surely then, this wicked world which is so radically opposed to God, and under the present control of His arch enemy, is not growing better. On the contrary, judgment, fire, and perdition are before it. (2 Pet. ii, 2-6; Jude vii; Mark ix, 43-48.) Perilous times are coming. (1 Tim. iv, 1.) "Evil men and seducers shall wax worse and worse, deceiving and being deceived." The tares, which naturally grow much faster than wheat, shall continue up to the harvest.   (Mat. xiii, 40.)

"The night is dark, the storms about us sweep
But Thou, O Lord, Thine own wilt surely keep;
Calm amid storm, secure through darkest night,
Thy Word our Lamp, a clear and steadfast light."

"Yet through the gloom, with yearning hearts we
    watch,
The first, faint promise of the dawn to catch;
With eager hope and glad expectancy,
That Thou, our risen Lord, we soon shall see."

"Come, blessed Morning Star, our hope, our all;
Come in Thy brightness, Thy redeemed to call,
Home to Thyself, that place of endless day,
The Father's house, our rest, eternally."

Rev A. T. Pierson in writing of the "Present Day Apostasy" says: "Modern church life is almost undermined by worldliness. To exagerate the extent of the evil and the danger, is scarcely possible. Between the church as a body, and the world, what clear line of definition and of separation exists except in the fact of church membership? The above fact is too well known to call forth even a doubt as to the appalling condition of the formal church. Paul in writing of the last great apostacy of the gospel age, clearly sets forth the fact that prior to the Coming of Jesus, there shall be a falling away from the faith. (2 Thess. i, 3.) This does not look like the triumph of the church in this present "Evil Age." Color it as we will, it is still evil and will continue to be so until the establishing of Christ's Kingdom in the Earth. Those who hold the optimistic view are in a sad plight when called to defend their position from a Bible point of view, because the Bible teaches just opposite from what they would have us believe.

W. E. Blackstone in his book "Jesus is Coming," sets forth the position of the Pre- and Post-Millennialist. We herewith give a few of the rich nuggets contained in the same: "Post-Millenialist seem to think that all must be accomplished under the church, and with present instrumentalities. Pre-Millennialists look for the main accomplishment under Christ Himself, who will cut the work short in righteousness, (Rom. ix, 28.) and with different instrumentalities." (Isa. iv, 4; Zec. xiv.)

Post-Millennialism exalts the Church; Pre-Milleninalism exalts Jesus and fills the heart of the believer with a Living, Personal, Coming Saviour.

The Authority of Scripture.

——✠——

A S We near the close of this "present evil age," we should not be surprised if the enemy of all righteousness does his worst to inject doubts into the minds of the children of men relative to the "Authority of Scripture." The advancement of the new thought movement is the vanguard of antagonism to the inspiration of Scripture. Hence we find that the Word of God is not readily recieved as authoritative. Private interpretations of all varieties are wide spread in the earth, thus the thousand and one factions are seeking to build their religious cob-houses, that will burn as stubble on the reckoning day. If, on the other hand, the sacred Scriptures are not authoritative, we should deify intellect and crowd God from our mind. But if the sacred Scriptures are authoritative, then we should look to them as the only court of appeal.

The one safe rule to follow is, to believe that God says what He means, and means what He says. This rule if put into practice, would bring a spirit of unity and fellowship that is so much needed in this "Present Evil Age." When the Scriptures tell us that we must be born from above in order to get into the Kingdom, we should believe it without any "talk back," for it is God's Word. It is not a question of what we think, but what God says. If He tells us in His Word that it is His will that we should be sanctified, and live holy lives, there is but one thing to do. Believe He means what He says, and go to Him for the accomplishment of His will. Doubt cannot live in an atmosphere of faith, and without faith it is impossible to please God. Thus we see that faith brings the favor of God. Should we read of God's judgments on sin and sinners, in the Bible, no matter how severe it appears, we should remember that God is a Sovereign and has a perfect right to punish those who rebel against Him and His government. If the punishment is said

48

to be "Hell Fire," there is but one thing to do—believe it. You may rest assured that God will make no mistake. Yea, the Judge of all the earth will do right.

The great sin of this "Present Evil Age" is seeking to twist the scriptures, in order to make them what is termed "common sense." If this be the case, who is the one to establish the standard? For each one with his "common sense" interpretation believes he has the right one. All such procedure is from the pit, and those who work along these lines are the devil's best agents. It is to the law and to the testimony, from which there is no appeal, that reference should be made.

Professor Muller, of Halle, says; "He who does not recognize the doctrine of justification by faith, and does not believe in the authority of the Bible, renounces the Protestant Church."

In 1523, the time of the first religious colloquy, the vicar of Constance, having proposed to refer it to the Universities of Paris, Cologne, or Lourain: "It is not necessary so to do," replied Zwingle, "we have here an impartial and infallible judge in the

49

Holy Scripture. It cannot lie, nor deceive."
And an adversary desiring to appeal to the
Fathers, he replied, 'It is not a question of
fathers or mothers, but of what is in accor-
dance with the Word of God."

To any one who is at all familiar with
the history of the Reformation, there is no
question why success crowned their efforts.
The instrument of war they used was the
"Word of God." Hence they enlisted Him
who gave the Word as their defence. Cal-
vin, in his letter to Cardinal Sadolet, wrote,
"The word of God alone is beyond the
sphere of our judgment," and in his "Anti-
dote to the Articles of the Theological Fac-
ulty of Paris," he says: "If a controversy
arise it should not be decided at man's
pleasure, but solely by the authority of
God. Since the world is at this time so
much troubled by a diversity of opinions,
there is no other remedy; we must find our
refuge in the Scriptures." It is so still.

Paul, in his pastoral epistles written to
Timothy, declares that ALL Scripture is
given by inspiration of God and is profitable. * * * This being a fact, we cannot lightly esteem any portion of the Holy
Writ.

Thus, those prophesies that point to the first and second advent are of profit to the child of God. The fact of His second coming is also a fact of prophesy, and is of as great importance to the Church, as His first coming was to the world. At this point we are brought face to face with that spirit of religious infidelity so prevalent in the world to-day. This spirit is detected by its indifference to the coming of Jesus and to His reign on earth.

The work of the anti-christ is to counterfeit as near as possible the real work of Christ, hence the confusion, as a large majority of professors are not sufficiently spiritual to discern the difference between the real and the counterfeit. Thus we hear such expressions as follow: "a side issue," "it causes divisions," "should not be preached," "let's hold to the main line," and a multitude of similar expressions which reveal the opposite spirit, to that of true Christianity.

The fact that we find mysteries beyond our depth, proves the divine origin of the sacred Word. He who dares trifle with God's Word will find it to be the instrument by which he will be judged. A man who kills his brother will have lighter punishment at the judgment, than he who attempts to kill *any portion* of God's Word. We are told that Heaven and earth shall pass away, but His Word shall not pass away. "Thus the Holy Scripture will be and remain in the richest and most sublime sense, the Book of Life." It will sustain itself in the face of all the development of human culture that the world can produce, and it will survive them all. One will no longer seek in Scripture, solutions for questions which only refer to science in its divers branches, or which pass beyond the limits of the human mind. (Col. ii, 18.) The Holy Scriptures will be the oracle for all that concerns the salvation of man—the oracle to teach us how all the different relations of life should be formed and directed, so that they may tend to and attain an eternal end. And practical exigencies will lead us to find this road."

In conclusion, we would say, in the language of D'Aubigne: "Do not be satisfied with receiving ready-made from the hands of others, what you yourself ought to find in the Scriptures; you must search it; you must find it; you must apply it. He who seeks well, finds well. Go beyond us, dear friends, but in the study of Scripture; go beyond us, we conjure you, but in the knowledge of this Word of God, in its application to your heart and life, in assurance of faith, in the fidelity with which you endeavor to bring before Christian people, not your own thoughts, but the thoughts of God Himself, as they are found in His oracles. For this end work, but with great humility, with great distrust of yourself. Work, remembering that you *'wrestle not against flesh and blood, but against spiritual wickedness in high places,'* against the influence of evil systems and the spirit of the times, against the seduction of the demons of pride and unbelief: *'withstand in the evil day, and having done all, stand.'* " May God grant this unto you!

The Voice of Judgment.

------ ✠ ------

THERE is no subject in the Bible from which the heart so naturally recoils, as that of the damnation of the unsaved. This may be one reason why so few are scripturally enlightened on this Bible doctrine. While it is not a pleasant subject to dwell upon, we are forced to give it the place that God designed it should fill in the ministry of His Word. If men will not listen to the voice of love, then they must listen to the *voice of judgment*. The love pleadings of a Father's heart have repeatedly impressed themselves upon your mind; yet you continue in the course of sin. Do you not see that ere long the race of life will be run, and you will confront the black catalogue of your personal sins, and that

54

there is no way to escape the final summing up of your misspent life? As truly as God has prepared a glorious kingdom for those who have accepted the ransom paid for their sins, just so truly is there a lake of fire and brimstone for those who have ignored the priceless redemption that Christ purchased for all The exquisite delights of the saved will have their great contrast in the most awful suffering imaginable, in the dark confines where murderers will try in vain to wash the blood stains of their victims from their hands. The blatant fool and religious infidel, who try to convince themselves and others that the Bible does not mean what it says, that Christ is a liar and fire is not hot, and all such hellish twaddle, will meet their just deserts where fire *is* hot, and the worm dieth not. The fact of Christ's death argues the displeasure of God against sin. He hates it. He cannot look upon it with any degree of allowance. It must be put away, or it will carry its victims to the place from whence travelers never return.

The hour of death is fast approaching the present generation, the majority of which have made no provision for the boatman to carry them over. The dark, cold waters of trouble and death, are beginning to gather about their feet. Oh! What dismay! Death has come, no hope, no friend, no comfort, no light, no joy, no peace, or rest. The past with its lost opportunities is before them. The tender appeal of loving hearts rings out afresh, only to be dashed against a heart of stone. Hush! the silence is broken. Look! Sitting bolt upright in bed, with hands waving frantically, the last earthly battle is being fought; the hands drop; the husky voice is heard to say, "Lost! Lost!" and with one despairing cry, that soul is carried forth by the weight of its own sin, to the infernal regions of everlasting despair.

> "How they deserve the deepest Hell
>   That slight the joys above!
> What chains of vengeance must they feel,
>   Who slight the bands of love!"

From the morning of thy earliest recollection, white robed mercy has been pleading with thy soul; but thou, in stubborn, wilful rejection, hast continued in open rebellion against the bleeding Lamb of Calvary. The devil has continued to satisfy the flesh with all the carnal pleasures in which the unregenerate revel. The dance hall, the theatre, the gambling table, and the house of shame have bidden for thy substance, and have obtained it. The race of life is nearly run; broken in health, the soul stumbles toward the burning pit. How different would have been the ending of this life had the soul turned from evil unto God. But, alas! it is too late! The opportunity has gone. Mercy has veiled her face, the door of hope is closed and darkness gathers as the eternal night comes on. How keen the sense of anguish; the soul now fully alive to its lost condition, experiences! What moments of remorse as the soul glides on toward its final abode! The tongues of a thousand demons have already begun to hiss in their glee because Christ has been robbed of another soul.

O sinner, consider the fearful danger you are in! It is a great furnace of wrath, a wide and bottomless pit, full of fire and brimstone, that you are held over in the hand of that God whose wrath is provoked and incensed as much against you, as against many of the damned in Hell. "However unconvinced you may be now, of the truth of what you hear, by and by you will be fully convinced of it." "Let every one that is out of Christ, and hanging over the pit of Hell, whether they be old men or women, or middle aged, or young people, or children, now hearken to the love calls of God's Word and providence. This acceptable year of the Lord, a day of great mercy to some, will doubtless be a day of as remarkable vengeance to others. Men's hearts will harden, and their guilt increases apace at such a day as this, if they neglect their souls. Never was there a period when so many means were employed for the salvation of souls, and if you entirely neglect them, you will eternally curse the day of your birth.

"Now, undoubtedly it is, as it was in the days of John the Baptist, the axe is laid at the root of the tree, and every tree which bringeth not forth good fruit, may be hewn down and cast into the fire. Therefore, let every one that is out of Christ, now awake and flee fron the wrath to come. The wrath of Almighty God is undoubtedly hanging over every unregenerated sinner. Let every one flee out of Sodom." *"Haste and escape for your lives, look not behind you, escape to the mountain lest you be consumed."*

The Golden Age.

———✠———

"THE Lord's Coming sustains such an exceedingly important relation to the whole scheme of redemption, that the enemy has taken special pains to prevert or obscure it; and in this he has been far too successful during the centuries of apostasy. If there is any one truth which should be kept before the people, it is the all important truth of *His Second Coming.*

Around this great and giorious truth, all other truths cluster. It is the star that out-shines all others. It tells us of the *Golden Age;* of a period of world wide righteous-ness, when the glory of the Lord will cover the earth as the waters cover the sea. Holi-ness may be unpopular in this wicked and adultrous generation, but there is coming a day when the blessed doctrine of Holiness will receive its due attention. Zechariah, in writing of that day, says: "There shall be upon the bells of the horses, Holiness unto the Lord." (Zech. xiv, 20.) The prophets, with their prophetic vision, waxed eloquent as they, under the inspiration of the Holy Ghost, portrayed the coming glory of Christ's kingdom on earth.

Isaiah, the royal prophet, seems to lead all others in his marvelous word-pictures of the literal reign of Christ upon the throne of His father David. He tells us of a time coming when "the wilderness and the solitary place shall be glad for them; and the desert shall rejoice and blossom as the rose." He also makes mention of the fact that "the glorious Lord will be unto us a place of broad rivers and streams; wherein shall be no galleys with oars, neither gallant ships pass thereby." "For the Lord is our Judge, the Lord is our Lawgiver, the Lord is our King."

According to the prophet Micah, the first and only unanimous peace conference will be held after Jesus establishes His universal

kingdom on earth.   Listen to the glowing
account he gives of that most desirable age.
"But in the last days it shall come to pass,
that the mountain of the house of the Lord
shall be established in the top of the mountains, and it shall be exalted above the
hills; and people shall flow unto it.   And
many nations shall come, and say, Come,
and let us go up to the mountain of the
Lord, and to the house of the God of Jacob;
and He will teach us of His ways, and we
will walk in His paths: for the law shall go
forth of Zion, and the Word of the Lord
from Jerusalem. And He shall judge among
many people, and rebuke strong nations
afar off; and they shall beat their swords
into plowshares, and their spears into prun-
inghooks: nation shall not lift up sword
against nation, neither shall they learn war
any more.   But they shall sit every man
under his vine and under his fig tree; and
none shall make them afraid: for the
mouth of the Lord of hosts hath spoken it."

We are not only confronted with the desirable truths as stated above, but we are
encouraged to look forward to a time when
the devil will be bound and shut up in the

bottomless pit. The language of John, as found in the twentieth chapter of Revelation, tells in no uncertain sound of the triumph of Christ over the devil. "And I saw an angel come down from Heaven, having the key of the bottomless pit and a great chain in his hand. And he laid hold on the dragon, that old serpent, which is the devil and Satan and bound him a thousand years, and cast him into the bottomless pit, and shut him up, and set a seal upon him, that he should deceive the nations no more, till the thousand years should be fulfilled; and after that he must be losed a little season." At this point we are brought face to face with a period of time when there will be no devil to tempt men into sin. Hence the *"Golden Age"* we hear so much about these days. The great *"World-wide Revival"* that has been talked threadbare will then take place, for a nation shall be born in a day.

May the precious Holy Ghost enable us to so live that, when the trump of God shall sound, we will be among those who will be "caught up to meet the Lord in the air, and so shall we ever be with the Lord." "Wherefore comfort one another with these words."

Towards the Great Divine Event.

BECAUSE of the transgression of the first Adam, God declared that the whole material creation should be subjected to a curse. (Gen. iii, 17.)

Thus, for the last six thousand years, man has eaten bread by the sweat of his brow; the earth also has brought forth thorns, thistles and briars. Man, the crowning work of creation, has been subjected to sorrow and countless other misfortunes. Disappointment, disease, and death have

64

marked his path from the fall to the present. The severe changes of climate are but a manifestation of God's displeasure against sin. The falling leaves and decayed branches are arguments of God's curse upon the earth. The bitter wail of the deserted infant tells the awful story of man's transgression. The parched tongue of the beast that roams our forest is but another sign of the dreadful calamity that befell the race because of our first parent's wilful act of disobedience. The birds of prey are a part of the great unwritten history that stretches out before us like the burning sands of the desert. The roar of the storm-tossed billows are but the inward groans of creation. Each tombstone silently preaches that death reigns. The tiniest petal that graces the bosom of mother earth adds its testimony to the thousands of other witnesses, that man is out of harmony with his God. The toiling bee and crushed insect add their humble evidence to prove the extent to which the curse of God has been felt. Each broken and bleeding blade of grass unites its voice in the proclamation that the day has not yet come, that creation has longed for. The mineral, vegetab'e and animal kingdoms, are unanimous in their testimony to the fact that discord and broken strings have taken the place of harmony and perfection. There is not a home in the land where the trail of the serpent is not seen: but we rejoice in the fact that in the near future the scene will be changed.

The second Adam is coming, and will restore all things to their proper sphere and place. Groaning and travailing creation will be delivered from the bondage of corruption into the glorious liberty of the sons of God. He who was crowned with thorns, will be crowned with glory and immortality; restoring all things. The long night of sin will have passed away: the morning of eternal glory will have been ushered in. The dark chapter of failure and defeat will have become history; the light of eternity will stream forth in fadeless splendor. The rough places will be made smooth, and the crooked places straight. Then shall the lame man leap as a hart, the eyes of the blind shall see, and the tongue of the dumb sing; for in the wilderness shall water break forth and streams in the desert. The

66

all-conquering Christ will take to Himself His great power and reign. The earth rulers shall throw their crowns at His feet, while He takes the sceptre of universal power and reigns from sea to sea. All the earth will be filled with His glory. There will be nothing to mar or molest in all His holy mountain, for the glory of the Lord will cover the earth as the waters cover the sea.

The animal kingdom will also be delivered: for the lion shall eat straw like the ox. All this is but the beginning of that complete redemption which Christ purchased for us in His atonement. "And it shall come to pass in that day, that the light shall not be clear, nor dark, but it shall be one day which shall be known unto the Lord, not day, nor night; but it shall come to pass, that at evening time it shall be light. And it shall be in that day that living waters shall go out from Jerusalem, half of them toward the former sea, and half of them toward the hinder sea; in summer and in winter shall it be. And the Lord shall be King over all the earth; in that day shall there be one

Lord and His name one." (Zech. xiv, 6-9.) "In that day shall there be upon the bells of the horses, *Holiness Unto the Lord.*"

The Image of God Restored.

———✠———

THE wise men of earth spend their time in searching for earthly wisdom. Those who would be wise unto salvation must search for divine wisdom in Christ, "For He is our wisdom." The value of heavenly wisdom cannot be compared to things of earth. Hence one must be in possession of it in order to realize its value. While the Angels are perfect in their obedience to the will of God, they can never know the inward illumination that divine wisdom imparts. That can only be experienced by those who were made in the image of God.

The Christ nature restored to the individual is the object for which He died. There is no higher plain of life possible than that of being filled with *"All the Fullness of God."* The Christ life is one of purity and obedience to our Father God. He who thus lives is satisfied. The three-fold nature of man brought under the perfect government of Heaven by the cleansing away of original sin is the image restored. This is the high calling and privilege of every child of God.

The worldly wise cannot fathom the depths of this most glorious experience. Hence they call in question the reality of such a life. But, he who has been made wise unto salvation, and has obtained by faith this state of inward rest and victory, has settled all questions so far as he is concerned. It has become an accomplished fact.

There is nothing in this life more desirable than perfect adjustment to circumstances and conditions. Victory over unfavorable environment can only be obtained as we enter 'the Sanctified life." This is the "White Stone," and the "New Name" of christian experience—"Sanctified wholly" in spirit, soul and body. Thus we are brought not merely into tune with the Infinite, but into the sweetest fellowship.

This is the highway, or the way within a way. The burning of the Omnipotent God scatters all darkness thus enabling the sanctified to walk in the light as He is in the light, with the inward knowledge that the Blood of Christ cleanseth from "All Sin." This blessed unity of trinity both in Heaven and on earth is the triumph of Christ's gospel in the individual heart.

This is the land of Canaan—the vast fields of perfect delight, where the inhabitants can eat bread without scarceness, and when they shall have eaten and are full then they will bless the Lord. This experience forever settles the carnal pleasures, and lifts the soul into such heavenly contemplations that nothing but Christ can satisfy.

The majestic realm of spiritual revelation is made possible when the soul enters into the marriage relationship with the Triune God. This state can only be realized by an absolute surrender to the perfect will of God—Dead to sin and self, and alive un-

71

to God for the glory of His Name. The most exquisite soul delight is thus enjoyed; when the trinity of man is in perfect accord with the Holy Trinity.

The Glory of Christ's Kingdom.

———✠———

IF There is one theme above another that thrills the hearts of all true believers, it is the majestic theme of Christ's Kingdom. The objective point of all christian experience is the final triumph with Christ in His glorious reign. Hence we are led to consider a few of the many prominent features that rise like mountain peaks covered with virgin whiteness.

Power: In Luke's gospel, the 21st chapter and 27th verse, we read; "And then shall they *See* the *Son of Man Coming* in a cloud with *Power* and great glory." This verse clearly sets forth the glorious fact of Christ's Triumph and Power; which He is going to exercise during His reign as King over the entire earth. This power will be seen is His judicial functions as He takes the Throne of His father David, and reigns from sea to sea. This power is not only seen in connection with the administration of righteous laws that pertain to His government on earth, but in the social, and religious world as well. In the fourth chapter of Micah and the fourth verse, we have a picture of true sociology that demonstrates the Power of Christ's influence over the nations that live during His righteous rule. We not only find this Power in the social world, but it extends in a far more glorious way religiously. Please observe the world-wide interest taken in the things that relate to man's highest and best interests. In the second verse of this same chapter, we read of a time coming when it will be a nation's desire that another nation will meet them in holy convocation. "And many nations shall come, and say, 'Come, and let us go up to the Mountain of the Lord, and to the house of the God of Jacob, and he will teach us of his paths: for the law shall go forth of Zion, and the word of the Lord from Jerusalem.'" There is no difficulty experienced in understanding such scriptures, when placed where the Holy Ghost puts them. We are not dealing with shadows, but substance. The Second Coming of Christ is as material as His first coming. Hence we find His kingdom to be a material kingdom. Thus it is that we are brought face to face with such marvelous manifestations of divine Power.

Blessing: If the withdrawing of Christ's spirit from the earth would be a calamity, then His personal presence would be a *Blessing*. This is just what is going to take place when He comes again. We will notice first His blessing in the family life. In the eighth chapter of Zechariah and the third verse, through to the eighth, we have a most profound truth set forth. That of national prosperity as seen in the family life. "Thus saith the Lord, I am returned unto Zion, and will dwell in the midst of Jerusalem: and Jerusalem shall be called a city of truth; and the mountain of the Lord of hosts, the holy mountain.. Thus saith the Lord of Hosts; there shall yet old men and old women dwell in the streets of Jerusalem, and every man with his staff in his hand for multitude of days. And the streets of the city shall be full of boys and girls playing in the streets thereof. Thus saith the Lord of hosts: If it be marvelous in the eyes of the remnant of this people in these days, should it a'so be marvelous in mine eyes? saith the Lord of hosts. Thus saith the Lord of hosts: Behold, I will save my people from the east country, and from the west country, and I will bring them, and they shall dwell in the midst of Jerusalem; and they shall be my people, and I will be their God, in truth and in righteousness."

What a contrast between the days spoken of in the scripture just quoted, and these evil days in which we live, when dogs have taken the place of children. and all manner of methods resorted to, to prevent life rather than to encourage it.

We not only find the Blessing of Christ in the matrimonial and family life, but also in the great animal kingdom. Isaiah the royal Prophet, with his prophetic vision, saw the majesty and blessing of Christ's kingdom in all its multiplied phases. He not only depicts in minute detail the righteous character of this golden age, but clearly sets forth in language easy to be understood, the wonderful change that will take place among the beasts of the field when Christ reigns as King. The 11th chapter of Isaiah contains a whole library in itself, setting forth Christ as the branch, as judge, and the great earth ruler. It not only deals with the office and work of Christ in relation to man, but His sovereign power over all creation. Thus we read: "The wolf also shall dwell with the lamb, and the leopard shall lie down with the kid; and the calf and the young lion and the fatling together: and a little child shall lead them; And the cow and the bear shall feed; their young ones shall lie down together; and the lion shall eat straw like the ox. And the sucking child shall play on the hole of the asp, and the weaned child shall put his hand on the adder's den. They shall not hurt or destroy in all my holy mountain; for the earth shall be full of the knowledge of the Lord as the waters cover the sea."

Signs of Christ's Speedy Coming.

——✠——

THERE is no truth in all the Bible that so warms our hearts as the one under consideration. It is our purpose to set forth a few of the many signs which precede His coming.

We desire first to call your attention to Dan. xi, 24: "Shut up the words and seal the book even to the time of the end; many shall run to and fro. and knowledge shall be increased." "A comparison of recent years with the present shows a most marvelous increase of both travel and knowledge." Railroads belt the earth, while mighty steamers fly like phantoms across the rolling deep. The ends of the earth are

78

brought together by telegraph wires, that continually transmit messages around the globe. Untold thousands are constantly running to and fro, from continent to continent, state to state, and from city to city. This is at least a fulfillment of the above prophecy. Note the increase in knowledge! Beautiful libraries, with their millions of books, speak for themselves that knowledge is on the increase. The average young man of twenty is better read to-day than was the man of fifty, twenty-five years ago. Schools of all classes and grades are springing up like a mighty forest throughout the earth. All this is but another fulfillment of the prophecy uttered twenty-five hundred years ago. Note! These prophecies were to be fulfilled in the *"time of the end."*

Another prophecy relating to our day is found in 2 Timothy, ii, 1: "This know also that in 'the last days' perilous times shall come." That these days are upon us is a fact too evident to be successfully refuted. Notice the progress of Nihilism, Socialism, Communism and Anarchy, together with the crushing money trusts and murderous labor unions, with the unrest of nations. They surely present a picture of perilous times.

All this is but a drop in the bucket, when we look into the mass of corruption that exists in the great social world as it stands today. Our daily papers are reeking with virus of the so-called cultured society. The mighty divorce scourge that is sweeping through our land like a prairie fire, and leaving in its wake death and damnation, is perilous in the extreme, in that it is wrecking the home life of our nation, and setting a prestige for the rising generation that will reap a harvest of bastards and help populate Hell by the thousand. The fact that men have the nerve to advocate "trial marriage" in this enlightened age, proves the deep undercurrent of unrestrained lust, that every now and then breaks out among the 'upper class.'"? These are among the leading sins that have characterized the close of each dispensation. Surely these are perilous times.

Another one among the many signs of the last days, is the *"distress of nations."* All Europe is one great soldiers' camp,

80

armed to the teeth, and ready to fly at each other in a universal war. There are over 23,000,000 drilled men that the governments have to support. Hence we easily find the cause of "distress of nations."

Notice again in 1 Timothy, iv, 1: "Now the Spirit speaketh expressly that in the latter times some shall depart from the faith, giving heed to seducing spirits and doctrines of devils." This is one of the definite signs of the times. One of the most subtle doctrines of devils, is that of Christian Science, "for, like Theosophy, it denies the atonement of Christ, and asserts that every man is his own Saviour." There are said to be more esoteric Buddhists in and about Boston than there are natives in Austria. Spiritualism, with its myriads of adherents, continues its "Gift of Tongues" to deceive the simple. And thus the dark clouds of latter day apostacy gather. The Post-Millennialists may, by fair speech and smooth words, rock some to sleep in their cradles of "peace, peace," but the Scriptures teach us that when they say peace and safety, then sudden destruction cometh.

"Oh, Church of Christ, behold at last
 The promised sign appear;
The Gospel preached in all the world
 And so the King draws near."

81

New Life In Jesus.

———✠———

THERE is no theme which has demanded so much attention as that of *Life*. As a matter of fact, the best brains are constantly employed to find out how life can be prolonged. But alas! how futile is all such research! In spite of man's mighty effort, death marches on,—claiming its victims. There is but one solution of this problem—namely, Christ. He alone is the Resurrection and the Life. All else has failed, and will continue to fail.

How glorious that in Christ there is Life, —new Life—Life more glorious, more complete than that of angels. This Life is not of the earth-nature, it is begotten by the Holy Ghost, and is identical with the Christ life. It is God's nature imparted. What heights of complete joy are experienced when this most blessed truth becomes a devine reality in the heart of the individual believer!

This *New Life* which has been begotten by the Holy Ghost has no relation to sin whatever; it is of Heaven, heavenly. Hence it feeds upon heavenly things. All this apology for committing sin is but an open acknowledgment of the supremacy of king carnality. *"Whosoever is born of God doth not commit sin."*

There is no difficulty in leading Christ's followers into the experience of Entire Sanctification. All this performance of teasing and coaxing men and women to get sanctified wholly is an open argument that you are dealing with unsaved people. From the moment of the New Birth, there is implanted in the soul a longing for heart purity, and no one ever refuses that for which he longs. This is the touchstone which proves the presence or absence of the New Life.

We have no quarrel with men who live moral lives, but they have no right to call that life the *Christ Life,* and here is where the fight rages. It is the master stroke of Satan to induce men to think that if they live a moral life that is all that is required of them. This might sound well if there was no Bible, which is our only court of appeal. It is not a question of *doing* in its negative form, but a question of *being* in its positive form. There are countless thousands who outwardly do right but are not inwardly right. Hence the Scripture, *"Man looketh on the outward appearance, but God looketh at the heart."*

The words of Christ to that noble ruler in Israel, *"Ye must be born from above,"* are as much in force to-day as when spoken. There is no argument that can stand before the burning words of the eternal Son of God. Kingdoms have risen and fallen according to the infallible Word of the living God. Not one jot or tittle will in any wise fail. *"Ye must be born from above."*

This is the exalted privilege of earth's millions, for He willeth the death of no man, but that all should come to repentance. This was the object of Christ's death upon the cross. He suffered that we might live. How soon this earth would become a Paradise if men would but obey the voice of Scripture!

Again, life in all forms in which we are acquainted with it, is progressive, small at the beginning, it advances to maturity. Thus we see that Christianity is not a stagnant pool, but a *living* stream, ever flowing onward and upward. The people of God go from strength to strength, perfecting Holiness in the fear of the Lord. It is natural, therefore, that Christians should show a glow of joy. Although joy is not the proper citerion of progress, of the divine life, it is as essential to its nature to be progressive as it is to the life of the body to increase in stature as it advances from childhood to maturity. *"The joy of the Lord is our strength."*

Inasmuch as God, from the genesis of time, designed to live in human temples, we are instructed by the Scripture that our bodies are the temples of the Holy Ghost. This being true, we can easily account for the wonderful illuminations of the soul when it is presenced with divinity.

"Thou of Life the fountain art—
Thou dost wash me white as snow;

85

NEW LIFE IN JESUS.

I'm content to dwell apart
  From all else, Thy love to know.
Blessed Sun of righteousness,
  I so love to look on Thee,
That my eyes are growing blind
  To the things once dear to me."

The Gracious Invitation.

———✠———

WHAT great rapture and sublime satisfaction, must have seized the hearts of the anointed ones, as man came forth from the hands of his Creator. Man is the only being that ever possessed the image of the invisible God. The highest position ever held by a created intelligence, was held by man. It seemed to be the thought of God, that man should occupy the highest possible position in the earth: The great animal kingdom was subject to His laws, and compelled to obey His voice. The great and mighty forests that beautifies the bosom of the earth was caused to grow for the benefit of man;—in fact all that was originally made, was for the sole purpose of magnifying God in His work of creation, and enabling man to enjoy the highest possible concep'ions of the Eternal One. The thought of divine communion is of such a sublime character that only a few ever come to know its heavenly sweetness. It is beyond the finite mind to comprehend what man might have been, had he continued to live in unbroken fellowship with the "Almighty." The grandeur of the everlasting mountains, with their rocky base, are no comparison to the beauty of man as he came forth in majesty and strength from the hand of the Everlasting Father. The deep blue sky with its thousands of sparkling stars, are no comparison to the unfading glory that would have bedecked the crown of immortal life, made for the brow of man. The fiery comets that travel through infinite space and cause the ether to expand as they spend their force in their mad flight, are but a faint picture of man in his fallen state. None but the Infinite can realize the awful depth to which man by transgression fell. Instead of glory and immortality resting upon his brow, there we find wounds and sores that tell us the awful story of sin's triumph, and man's fall. Sickness and death, coupled with all the unpleasant things that man is heir to, are but the faint suggestions of the inward corruption that exists in the unregenerate heart.

Notwithstanding these deplorable facts, a "Gracious Invitation" has gone forth, inviting all to come to the fountain of living waters, whereby all may be healed;—yea cleansed from all the polutions of sin. Habits of every kind that is displeasing to God, can be broken; for the Lion of the Tribe of Judah hath prevailed. We would encourage all who wish to be delivered from the bondage of sin and its awful consequences, to accept the Gracious Invitation—"Come unto me all ye that are weary and heavy laden and I will give you rest." There is no other way of deliverance. The blood of Christ is the all-sufficient remedy for sin; all else will fail. You must get the victory over sin, or, sin will get the victory over you, and send your soul to a devil's hell. It is "Repent or Perish!" "Turn or burn!" Which shall it be?

Eternity! Eternity!
How long art thou, Eternity!

THE GRACIOUS INVITATION.

And yet to thee time hasts away,
Like as the war-horse to the fray,
Or swift as courriers homeward go,
Or ship to port, or shaft from bow.
    Ponder, O man, Eternity!

    Eternity! Eternity!
How long art thou, Eternity!
How terrible art thou, in woe,
How fair where joys forever glow.

God's goodness sheddeth gladness here,
His justice there wakes bitter fear.
    Ponder, O man, Eternity!

FINIS.

Pillar of Fire

A Journal Whose Object is to Proclaim a Full Salvation for Spirit, Soul, and body.

PUBLISHED MONTHLY

Office:
39 Bank Street,
North Attleboro, Mass.

Subscription Price

50 Cents Per Year.

Tracts

We Publish Thousands of Small Tracts, That Are Being Scattered All Over The United States and Canada. Send Free-Will Offering For A Package To Distribute.

PILLAR OF FIRE,   North Attleboro, Mass.

Books

We Carry A Good Line of Religious Books, Also

Bibles and Wall Mottoes

Wanted

Agents To Handle Our Publications.   Write For Terms,

Address

PILLAR OF FIRE,   North Attleboro, Mass.

PRESS OF NORTH ATTLEBORO CHRONICLE JOB PRINT

www.ingramcontent.com/pod-product-compliance
Lightning Source LLC
Chambersburg PA
CBHW020512030426
42337CB00011B/356